180 Days of
Manners

by

Donna B. Forrest, Ed.S., L.P.C

&

Jenny Menger

© 2007, 2005, 2003 by
YouthLight, Inc.
Chapin, SC 29036

Project Editor Susan Bowman
Layout by Tonya Daugherty

ISBN 1-889636-55-X
Library of Congress Catalog Number 2003101957

10 9 8 7 6 5 4 3
Printed in the United States of America

P.O. Box 115 · Chapin, SC 29036
(800) 209-9774 · (803) 345-1070
(803) 345-0888 · Email YL@youthlightbooks.com

Dedication

This book is dedicated to an amazing lady – one who was an outstanding teacher and one who touched many lives during her long career. She is one who always sets a wonderful example for those in her presence, as well as one who encourages and entertains people from a variety of places and professions. She is lovely, kind, compassionate, and inspirational to everyone. She is very unassuming, would feel undeserving of this praise – when in fact -- no one deserves it more!

Mrs. Betty Menger is the mother of four – one of whom is the co-author of this book. She daily exhibits the character traits and manners that are appreciated in all walks of life and in cultures all around the world!

We love you, and thank you -- as do all of those who have the pleasure of knowing you! You are truly an inspiration!

Our love,
Jenny and Donna

Acknowledgments

Thanks to the wonderful administration, faculty, staff, students and families that we have the pleasure of working with daily at Merriwether Elementary School in North Augusta, South Carolina!

Thanks to Abby, Lilly, and Emma who make us smile and dutifully sat while this book was written (and when they didn't were taught "manners")!

Thanks to our friends for the laughter and fun that keep us focused!

Table of Contents

Introduction i

Foreword v

Manners In General ....Days 1-9

Manners In The Classroom ....Days 10-36

Packing For A Field Trip ....Days 37-50

Assembly & Special Programs ....Days 51-55

Manners Around The School ....Days 56-69

Lunchroom Manners ....Days 70-78

Table Manners ....Days 79-89

Manners At Home ....Days 90-114

Manners All Around ....Days 115-130

Giving And Receiving Gifts ....Days 131-136

In Your Neighborhood..............................Days 137-146

Good Manners In The USA ....Days 147-151

Good Character ....Days 152-180
About the Authors

Introduction

This book is intended to be used by parents, teachers, scout leaders, and any positive adult role model working with our youth. Manners are the basis for exhibiting respect for self and others as well as an essential life skill as individuals progress throughout every stage of life.

This book is not intended as a complete curriculum or as a replacement or add-on to other curriculum areas. Manners build, as does character, on academic and social areas that are necessary to become successful individuals. A perfect score of 1600 on the SAT may be considered exceptional academically. But, we must consider the questions, "How would that bright young mind function without basic good manners and good character? What positive contributions to society and our world might be inhibited without the ability to respect self and others through the practice of good manners?"

The 21st century has seen many changes – some for the better and some that need improvement. One thing that should remain consistent is the instructing of our children in good manners. It is apparent that our current world situation needs peace and harmony promoted in every possible way. This begins with our children at very young ages in the home, school, and community. Positive adult role models are needed so that good character and manners are a way of life that our children witness and consider normal.

The daily statements in this book can be used in various ways throughout the home, school, community, and world. Some of these ways include:

- Journal entries in the Language Arts curriculum;

- Social Studies lessons that involve customs of various cultures;

- Reading / Literature assignments when discussing both good and not so good manners exhibited by characters within stories;

- Boy / Girl Scout projects;

- School-to-Work transition activities (i.e., mock business luncheon to practice table manners, etc.);

- Manners needed in public places such as stores, businesses, restaurants, etc.;

- Manners necessary in the home to promote a calmer environment with family; and,

- Many more ....!

Each of the daily ideas and thoughts are meant to help our children – the future of our world – focus on the meaning of good manners – not just at the table or specific identified places, but in EVERY area and function of our daily lives!

Manners
In General

Good Manners = Good Results

* When you use good manners, others form a good opinion of you.

* Good manners help everyone work better together.

* Good manners involve good choices.

Good manners are needed in the classroom, around school, at home, in stores, in restaurants, and everywhere!

✱ When everyone in the class and at school practices using good manners, the whole building is more orderly, friendly, and fun!

✱ Good manners at home really improve meals and family time!

✱ In stores and restaurants, good manners by you are noticed by adults and the reward – many times – are smiles and compliments!

Good manners are kind and respectful actions toward others and yourself.

* Waiting by the door for older people to enter the room first shows respect and kindness by you.

* "Please" and "Thank You" are nice words for friends as well as adults and show respect for others.

* Listening patiently helps you learn more and shows kindness and respect by you for those around you.

Good manners are needed by everyone.

* Government officials, like the President, must use good manners at all times and with all people.

* Parents and Grandparents need good manners on their jobs, in public places, and with family members.

* Teachers and Principals show respect for adults and students within the school by using good manners.

* Friends need good manners with each other in order to get along well.

Hurtful teasing is not good manners.

✱ Name calling is unkind.

✱ Jokes that hurt others feelings are not funny.

✱ Making fun of someone's family is mean.

Good manners are
basic character traits.

❋ Good manners show respect.

❋ Good manners are our responsibility.

❋ Good manners show just how special you are!

Good manners are needed in our world today.

* Good manners promote peace.

* Good manners promote harmony.

* Good manners promote equality.

Good manners help you be the best you can be!

* Good manners make you a better student.

* Good manners make you a better friend.

* Good manners make you a better family member.

Good manners make you a better you!

❋ Good manners are YOUR choice.

❋ Good manners show you care.

❋ Good manners build better character.

Manners
In The
Classroom

Raise your hand and wait to be called on before speaking.

* Share speaking and listening times.

* Listen to others when they speak as you would like them to listen to you when you speak.

* Remember – interruptions have no place in the classroom!

Day 10

Be respectful of the ideas of others.

* Laughing at someone who gives a wrong answer is not polite. Remember, we are all in school to learn so we don't always know the right answer first.

* New ideas deserve respect. For example, when Henry Ford had the "new idea" of a motorized car, do you think his friends ever dreamed of the Ford Motor Company as it is today?!

* Everyone likes to be heard.

Good manners respect
our emotional differences.

✱ Respect and CELEBRATE our different thoughts and ideas.

✱ Some of us cry when we are happy or sad – others get quiet – and others need to talk.

✱ We are emotionally different and we need to respect this in each person!

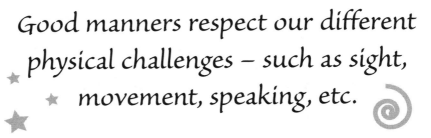

Good manners respect our different physical challenges – such as sight, movement, speaking, etc.

❋ Our former United States President, Franklin D. Roosevelt, spent most of his life in a wheelchair and think about how much he contributed to our nation!

❋ A former King of England had trouble speaking due to a stutter.

❋ Helen Keller's life has served as an inspiration and encouragement to many who are unable to see, hear or speak.

Your attitude is your choice.

❋ You can choose to obey rules and understand they are made in the best interest of all.

❋ You can choose to cooperate and share with a smile.

❋ You can choose to think good thoughts and discard bad ones.

Remember -
the SUCCESSFUL ATTITUDE
is the POSITIVE ATTITUDE.

* You know you can do some things well. Concentrate and practice those things.

* Set a short-term goal and believe you can reach it by working hard.

* Look at your blessings such as (your friends, teacher(s), counselor(s), parent(s), family, etc.) go to them for encouragement to keep a positive attitude.

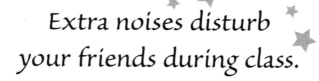

Extra noises disturb your friends during class.

❋ Singing or humming should be saved for music class!

❋ Your unnecessary noises usually "tells" the teacher and your classmates that you are not listening.

❋ Extra noises keep others from concentrating, which means no one is able to do their best.

Remain quiet when others are still working.

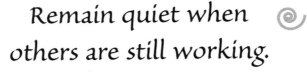

* If you finish early, enjoy the time to read or relax.

* If you finish early, you have time to check your work for careless errors.

* Pesty or peaceful, noisy or nice – the choice is yours!

Take good care of classroom materials.

✻ If you abuse it – you loose it! (If something is broken, torn, or lost, it is no good to you or anyone else.)

✻ Even if you don't plan to use it again, your classmates may need it (such as books, scissors, crayons, etc.).

✻ Be respectful of the money that was spent to buy these classroom materials – there may not be money to buy more.

Always return classroom materials to the proper place.

* Realize others may want to use those materials.

* It is good manners to clean up after yourself.

* This helps the classroom stay in order.

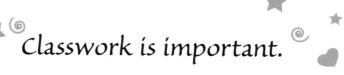

Classwork is important.

* Your classwork is your responsibility.

* Your work is a reflection of you.

* Do your best the first time!

Talk and visit at the proper times.

* Talk and visit with your friends at lunch or recess.

* Talk and visit with your teacher at lunch, recess, or special times during the day.

* During classwork there is no time for extra talking or visiting – that is a time to stay on task!

During school announcements, listen well.

✻ There are events that your friend or classmate may need to hear about even if you do not!

✻ Special instructions for the school day or after school may be something you and others in the class need to hear.

✻ There may be announcements of meetings or special events that you need to tell your parents about when you get home.

Remember to share and be patient.

❋ Good manners involve sharing with others things they may not have or may need to borrow – no one enjoys being around a selfish person!

❋ Learning to be patient is like learning to show good manners – it involves practice!

❋ Don't you want others to share and be patient with you?

Use respectful words and tone of voice when speaking to your teacher.

* It's not WHAT you say, but HOW you say it!

* You can be honest without being rude.

* If we are not careful, our words or the tone of our voices can make others feel uncomfortable – angry, hurt, sad, etc.

Good manners involve good, positive body language!

✽ ACTIVE listening involves LOOKING at the speaker to show that you are interested in what he/she is saying.

✽ In order to show respect with your body, there is no room to shrug shoulders or roll your eyes when someone speaks.

✽ Smiling or nodding to show you are listening encourages the person speaking or looking toward you.

When someone visits your classroom, remember to remain quiet and polite.

* Visitors deserve your respect.

* Visitors may feel uncomfortable in your classroom, so they need to feel welcome – you may wish to look at them and smile – but being quiet allows the teacher to direct the visitor to the proper place, etc.

* Your classroom is your "family" within the school... help leave a good impression on visitors!

During classroom treat time or parties, remember your good manners.

❋ "PLEASE" and "THANK YOU" are music to your teacher or parent volunteer's ears!

❋ If you don't like a "treat" or "snack", simply say, "Thank you, but I don't care for any." (NEVER say, "I don't like that!")

❋ Wait for your teacher to ask if you would like more – remember – the teacher can only do that if enough is left for everyone to have second servings!

Always cover your coughs or sneezes.

* Coughs and sneezes can be contagious – just like colds or flu – and can make others sick.

* Sickness is the one thing that we should never share!

* Germs can spread faster than peanut butter!

♥ *Kindness on your face shows kindness in your heart.*

❋ Smiling to encourage another person, shows a kind heart.

❋ Nodding to show someone you understand, is a kind reaction to that person.

❋ See the world through eyes that care – as you would like for others to look at you.

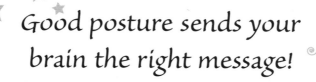

Good posture sends your brain the right message!

✱ Sitting up straight tells your brain that you are ready to learn!

✱ Putting your head down and slumping in your chair tells your brain to relax and "go to sleep".

✱ Good posture – or a "good listener" position – lets your teacher know that you are "all ears" – and your brain will connect with your teacher's instructions!

Neatness is NEAT!

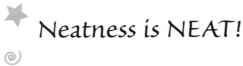

❋ N ever do a sloppy job – it reflects your effort!

❋ E veryone should be able to read your writing!

❋ A lways do your best – the FIRST time!

❋ T rust this fact – teachers love neat work!

In the mornings get ready for your day quickly and quietly.

❋ Mornings (beginnings) "set the tone" for the rest of your day.

❋ Organize your desk and sharpen your pencils BEFORE any "extra" talking to friends that your teacher or time might allow.

❋ Be ready to start when your teacher is ready to start – don't slow down the whole class – time is precious.

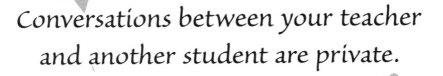

Conversations between your teacher and another student are private.

❋ Show your respect for others by focusing on your own work.

❋ Everyone needs private time – wait your turn (remember – patience).

❋ Sometimes a classmate may need the teacher and be embarrassed for others to hear their question or problem – your respect for this will be appreciated.

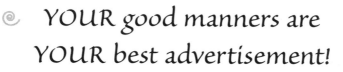

YOUR good manners are YOUR best advertisement!

* Your manners should "sell" your personality as being polite and, hopefully, others will want to "buy" a similar mannerism!

* The way you act through your manners let's other people see the real you – how do you want to be seen?

* Good manners lead to a good reputation (the way people will remember you five years from now).

Respect your teacher's space.

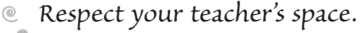

* Your desk holds your property, just as your teacher's desk holds your teacher's property.

* Only use or touch your teacher's materials if you have asked your teacher for permission first.

* If you see that your teacher is working at his/her desk – for example, with another student or on paperwork – wait to approach the teacher's desk until you have been invited.

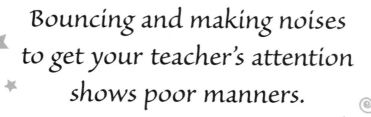

Bouncing and making noises to get your teacher's attention shows poor manners.

✳ Patience – or waiting your turn – shows good manners.

✳ Noises may bother or distract classmates and your teacher.

✳ Bouncing in your seat or waving your hand and making noises do not usually get good results – a better way might be to raise your hand and look at your teacher in his/her eyes to get attention.

Packing For
A Field Trip
With Manners

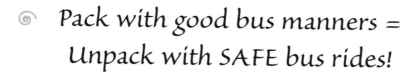

Pack with good bus manners = Unpack with SAFE bus rides!

❋ Good manners on the bus use quiet voices – loud voices can distract the bus driver and cause accidents.

❋ Good manners – as well as safety – include staying in your seat and in your space on the bus.

❋ Say "Thank You" to your bus driver.

Pack patience upon arrival.

❊ Good manners include waiting your turn to get out of your seat into the bus aisle to exit (never push or shove – someone could get hurt).

❊ Be orderly – LISTEN for directions.

❊ Once you are off the bus, remain in a quiet line until your teacher instructs the class.

Pack politeness and respect.

* Remember – you are the guest (or visitor). Your good manners will help you – and your class – to be invited back!

* Let your guide do the talking and lead the way – this helps you learn about the place you are visiting – as well as show off your good manners!

* Respect all field trip chaperones who volunteer to go with your class.

Communicate with your adult chaperones/teacher on the field trip.

✳ Ask permission to leave the group for any reason (i.e., use the restroom, get a drink of water, etc.)

✳ Use a respectful, kind tone of voice when speaking to your chaperone or teacher (there is no place for shouting or talking while someone else is talking).

✳ Raise your hand to ask questions while in the group (just as you do in the classroom).

Remember – you represent yourself and your school!

✳ The way you act often speaks your thoughts.

✳ When you and your classmates obey the rules, others will enjoy visits from your school.

✳ Smile often...your face will "say" good things.

🌀 Neatness in all places
is a form of manners.

✹ Be sure your shirt is tucked in.

✹ Be sure your shoelaces are tied.

✹ Your lunch box should be clean on the outside.

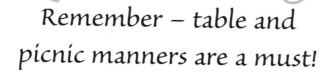

Remember – table and picnic manners are a must!

🌸 Your napkin should be in your lap.

🌸 Ask for food to be passed to you – don't reach.

🌸 Even when eating outside, use a soft, conversational voice.

Clean all litter.

* Help make sure no trash is left on or around the table.

* Be sure to clean up all food scraps.

* When throwing trash away, be sure it goes INSIDE the trash can.

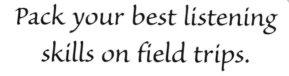

Pack your best listening skills on field trips.

* Listening will help keep you safe.

* Listening will let you know where to go and what to do.

* Listening will help you be SURE of a good day and a safe return home!

Remember – please and thank you are important words on field trips!

❋ Use please and thank you with your chaperones and teachers.

❋ Use please and thank you with your friends and students from other schools who may be visiting .. t.he same place.

❋ Use please and thank you with the people who are your guides or leaders.

Good manners include staying in your personal space on field trips.

* This is important for safety – roll calls, group calls, or counts.

* Rough play or pushing and shoving happens when you are out of your personal space (and can be dangerous).

* Staying in your personal space helps you have a nicer day.

Stay with your group and assigned chaperone.

* NEVER talk to strangers.

* You could get lost in a strange place.

* You might miss a fun activity.

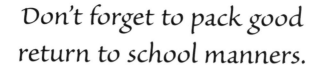

Don't forget to pack good return to school manners.

❋ Loading the bus should be done in an orderly fashion.

❋ Say "Thank You" to field trip guides or instructors.

❋ Return to your school building with quiet voices (remember—other classes may be working since they did not get to enjoy your trip).

"Thank You" notes are special.

* *Write a "Thank You" note to your chaperone(s).*

* *Write a "Thank You" note to your field trip guide or instructor.*

* *Write a "Thank You" note to your teacher.*

Assembly & Special Program Manners

Sit properly so those around you can see.

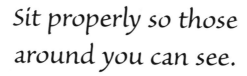

❋ Sit with your back straight.

❋ Sit with your feet on the floor.

❋ Face the speaker or stage.

Keep hands and feet in your personal space.

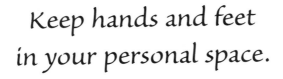

* Keeping hands and feet in your personal space helps you pay attention and learn more.

* This keeps others from disturbing you.

* This is usually a school rule – so let's obey!

Listen and follow instructions during special programs.

❋ "Hold your applause" means to wait until the end of the program to clap.

❋ Be an "active listener", so you can be a part of the program. This means listening with your eyes and ears.

❋ Your focus (or attention) should be on the speaker at all times.

Respect for the speaker, presenter, or performer = good manners.

❋ There is no place for rude noises (such as boos, etc.).

❋ Remember – the speaker or performer may be nervous. Think how you would feel in front of a room full of people.

❋ Talking to your friends during the performance is not good manners.

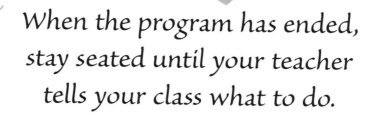

When the program has ended,
stay seated until your teacher
tells your class what to do.

* Jumping up confuses others.

* Everyone must leave orderly by taking turns.

* Your teacher is listening and watching for
instructions. Help her by staying seated and quiet.

Manners
Around
The School

Remember – other classes
are sometimes working
when you are in the hall.

✳ Hallways should be quiet places.

✳ Noises belong on the playground – not in the hall.

✳ Looking into other classrooms is distracting.

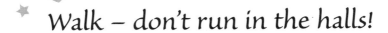

Walk – don't run in the halls!

❋ You could slip on the floor and hurt yourself.

❋ You might run into a smaller child if you were not walking.

❋ Hallways are the "streets" of the school... remember to stay safe by walking.

Holding doors for others is the right thing to do.

* Trying to always be first can cause problems.

* Adults will appreciate you holding the doors for them and allowing them to go first.

* Holding doors is helpful for those with physical challenges (crutches, wheelchairs, etc.)

Be kind to new students.

❋ Think about how you would feel if you were the "new kid on the block".

❋ Being kind will help you make a new friend.

❋ This is a good chance to show others your true good character.

Be a helper.

* Offer to help when someone accidentally drops something.

* Offer to help if you see someone with their arms full.

* Let a teacher know if you ever see another student being bullied.

Good manners are EVEN important at RECESS!

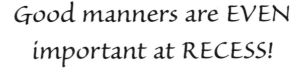

❋ Others want to play with you if you play fair which is using good manners with your friends.

❋ Taking turns at recess is good manners.

❋ Good manners at recess help everyone stay safe.

Being late makes others wait.

* Be ready and orderly when it's time for your class to go places.

* When it is time for school to be over, have your homework written down and your book bag packed so others do not have to wait on you.

* You don't want to be known as the "slow-poke".

Running errands is a privilege – practice good manners.

❋ Be responsible for the items you are delivering.

❋ Practice good manners when entering the school office on an errand.

❋ Knock politely and wait patiently if the errand is to another classroom.

Making a clean sweep
with good manners.

* Use good manners with school custodians.

* Respect the hard work the school custodians do.

* Say "Please" and "Thank You" to the school custodians.

Write on paper, not walls.

* Good manners respect school property.

* Writing on the walls is not nice for anyone to see.

* Writing on the walls makes extra work for school citizens and can cost a lot of money.

Terminate the litterbugs with good manners.

* Set a good example by picking up extra litter.

* Let others see you using the trash cans – not the floor.

* Make litterbugs EXTINCT!

"Check out" good manners in the library.

❋ Good book worms take care of all books.

❋ Turn in books on time so others can enjoy them also.

❋ Use a quiet voice at all times in the library.

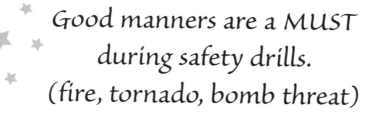

Good manners are a MUST during safety drills.
(fire, tornado, bomb threat)

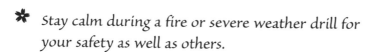

✱ Stay calm during a fire or severe weather drill for your safety as well as others.

✱ Follow directions carefully – it is not play time.

✱ Don't panic – be patient.

Good Sportsmanship = Good Manners

* Be fair.

* Be honest.

* Be a good winner as well as a good looser –
  no one can win all the time.

Lunchroom
Manners

Entering the lunchroom in a quiet
and orderly way shows good manners.

❋ Walk in a quiet line.

❋ "Cutting" in line is not "cool".

❋ An orderly line is a faster line.

Be polite to the workers in the cafeteria.

✳ Say "Please" and "Thank You".

✳ Be patient and wait to be served.

✳ Be courteous and respectful. They work very hard.

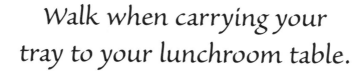

Walk when carrying your tray to your lunchroom table.

* Walking prevents accidents – such as dropping your food.

* Take your time – the cafeteria is a busy place.

* While in the cafeteria, walking is the ONLY safe and polite choice.

Sit properly at the lunchroom table.

* Good posture shows good manners.

* Sitting properly helps you stay in your own personal space.

* Sitting properly = Cleaner clothes! (Standing while eating is not good manners.)

Use a quiet voice while at the lunchroom table.

* You don't need to shout to be heard.

* A calm environment helps digest food better.

* In the lunchroom crowd, don't be loud!

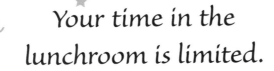

Your time in the lunchroom is limited.

❋ Be sure to pick up all food and other items you may need while you are in the line (then you won't waste time by having to go back).

❋ Eat first, then visit.

❋ Lunchrooms are for eating – not playing.

Your lunchroom table manners say a lot about you!

❋ Keep food separated on your tray.

❋ Leave the food you do want in place on your tray.

❋ Never throw food – that's the worst manners!

Eat your own lunch.

✱ Be polite – don't ask for someone else's food.

✱ Let YOUR fingers touch only YOUR food.

✱ Remember -- everyone is hungry at lunchtime!

Clean up when finished.

✻ When leaving the table, it is good manners to clean around your tray.

✻ Check the floor under your seat to make sure you haven't dropped anything.

✻ Your tray should be disposed of in the proper place.

Table
Manners

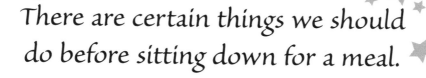

There are certain things we should do before sitting down for a meal.

* Always wash your hands before eating.

* Try to have a neat appearance by combing your hair and washing your face.

* Toys and games should be left in another place.

Hands, elbows, and napkins have their place.

* As much as possible, keep one hand in your lap.

* Elbows should be close to your side and never on the table.

* Napkins should be unfolded and placed in your lap when you first sit down.

Cool "C.A.T."s at the table use good manners.

* C hew your food quietly – smacking is not cool.

* A lways chew with your mouth closed.

* T alk only after you have swallowed your food.

Good table manners – never leave them behind!

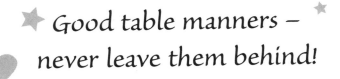

❋ When visiting a friend, use good table manners.

❋ When traveling, take them with you, too.

❋ Remember – set an example – others watch you at the table.

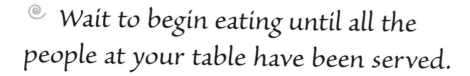

Wait to begin eating until all the people at your table have been served.

* At home, when the family is eating together, wait until everyone has their food.

* When eating at someone else's house, wait until everyone has been seated to begin eating.

* When eating in a restaurant, wait until those people at your table have received their orders before beginning to eat.

Choosing polite actions over greedy actions says good things about your manners.

✱ Take small to medium size portions of food.

✱ Wait to be offered a second helping.

✱ Pass the food – never reach or grab!

The table is a special place to use consideration and kindness.

* If you do not like a type of food, simply say, "No thank you."

* Talk only about pleasant subjects – things that anyone would like to hear.

* "Excuse me" is what to say if you must leave the table before everyone has finished the meal.

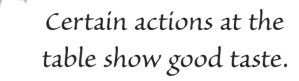

Certain actions at the table show good taste.

* Cover your mouth or nose with your napkin if you must cough or sneeze.

* Eat only the food on your plate – never take samples from someone else's plate.

* If you do not like the taste of something, cover your mouth with your napkin and place the bite of food in it.

A meal is to be enjoyed – take your time when eating.

❋ Let food "slide" into your mouth – never bite the fork or spoon when eating.

❋ Take small bites and chew your food completely.

❋ Take polite sips of your drink – never GULP!

There is a proper way to use each utensil (fork, spoon, knife).

❋ Hold utensils in your fingers – not your fist.

❋ After using your knife, lay it across the edge of your plate (not on the table).

❋ Utensils are for eating – not pointing.

Good manners appreciate the person who prepared the meal.

* Good manners never ask, "What is this?"

* Good manners say, "Thank you".

* Good manners say, "I enjoyed it."

Manners
At Home

(general—neighbors, parents,
siblings, guests, phone, possessions)

Make good manners a part of your family.

✱ You set a good example by showing your good manners.

✱ Listen to the ideas of your family members even if these ideas may be different than your own.

✱ Talk to family members with a kind tone of voice.

Model good manners at home...yes! Even with your sisters and brothers.

✳ Say "Please", "Thank You", and "Excuse Me" to your sisters and brothers just like you do to others.

✳ Ask before borrowing your sister or brother's clothes or toys.

✳ Be respectful of your sister or brother's personal space. Ask before entering!

"Please" and "Thank You" are special words to use at home, TOO!

* Your parents will appreciate hearing those words.

* "Please" and "Thank You" usually get you GOOD attention and better results.

* It's not WHAT you say, but HOW you say it.

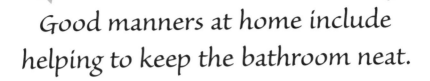

Good manners at home include helping to keep the bathroom neat.

* Place your towels and washcloths in the proper places when finished.
* Wipe up any spills or wet spots from the shower on the floor to help prevent accidents.
* Place your toothbrush and toothpaste in the correct area when finished brushing your teeth.

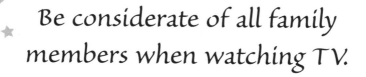

Be considerate of all family members when watching TV.

❋ Flipping channels in the middle of someone else's TV program is rude.

❋ Try to walk around the person instead of between the person and TV when a family member is watching a certain show.

❋ Keep your voice down so the TV can be heard.

Be considerate of those who want to use the computer.

❋ Work out a schedule if several family members want to use the computer.

❋ Learn to compromise or share computer time.

❋ School work should be done first on the computer – before games.

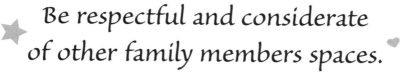

Be respectful and considerate of other family members spaces.

✳ Knock before entering if the door is closed.

✳ Ask permission before borrowing something that belongs to someone else.

✳ If you borrow something, it should be returned to the proper place.

Do your part to take care of family belongings.

* Cleaning shoes when entering the house keeps floors looking nice and neat.

* Furniture is expensive and belongs to everyone in the family – help take care of it.

* Food containers and refrigerator doors should be closed properly after use.

Everyone in the family has a special job to do.

* If everyone does his or her chores the first time, it leaves more time for play.

* Take care of your chores because that is your responsibility.

* Do your chores with a good attitude to the best of your ability.

Keeping family members waiting is inconsiderate.

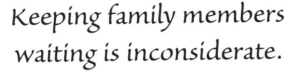

* Come to the table when you are called.

* Be ready on time.

* Be organized in advance so you will be ready.

Telephone manners are important, too.

* When answering the phone, use a clear, polite speaking voice.

* If the phone call is not for you, simply say, "May I ask who is calling?"

* Gently lay the telephone down and go find the person asked for... please do not yell.

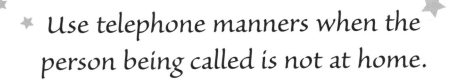

Use telephone manners when the person being called is not at home.

✽ If the person being called is not at home, ask, "May I take a message please?"

✽ Write the message down and remember to give it to the proper person.

✽ It is not polite to ask, "What do you want?"

Wait your turn when playing games.

* Practice patience.

* Be willing to share.

* Be a good sport.

Play fair.

* Fairness means being honest and respectful.

* Fairness means being a good winner as well as a good loser.

* Playing fair involves being kind.

The tone of your voice is always YOUR choice.

* A loud voice may make someone think you are angry.

* A soft, gentle voice calms those around you.

* Speak to others in the tone you wish them to speak to you.

Use your hands for helping, not hurting.

* Being polite never involves pushing or shoving.

* Being polite never involves hitting someone else.

* Being polite never involves hurting someone else's property or possessions.

Being polite means taking care of things parents have bought or provided for you.

* It's good manners, as well as good safety, to pick up toys and other belongings when you are finished with them.

* Your toys and clothes will last longer if YOU are responsible for them.

* Put things you have used back in their proper places.

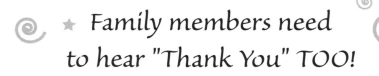

Family members need to hear "Thank You" TOO!

* Good manners include saying "thank you" for a meal.

* It is polite to say "thank you" to a family member who has done things for you (such as doing your laundry, etc.)

* Say "Thank You" when your parents have given something to you.

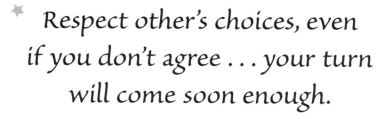

Respect other's choices, even if you don't agree . . . your turn will come soon enough.

✳ It cannot always be your turn.

✳ A pleasant attitude, even when you do not agree, helps everyone.

✳ Not everyone is supposed to think alike.

Think of your family as a team and you as an important part of that team.

❋ Everyone has feelings.

❋ Doing your part helps make a winning team (family).

❋ Being a good team player is important when some rough days occur.

Your actions are a mirror of YOU.

* Your actions reflect the kind of person you really are!

* Act toward others as you would like them to act toward you.

* Actions on the outside reflect the person on the inside.

Bathroom manners are important.

✱ It is polite to pick up after yourself
  (wet towels, clothes, etc.).

✱ If you spill shampoo, toothpaste, etc.
  it is nice to cleanup after yourself.

✱ Leave the bathroom for others as
  you would like to find it.

Be careful of noise when family members are resting.

* Open and close doors quietly.

* Use an "inside" voice.

* Keep the television and stereo soft.

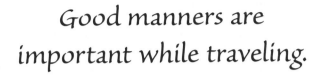

Good manners are important while traveling.

❋ Space is limited – stay in your personal space.

❋ It is good manners to take turns for certain seats in the vehicle.

❋ It is good manners to talk softly when traveling.

It is good manners to show respect
for the older people in the family
(like grandparents, aunts, or uncles).

❋ Listen first, talk later.

❋ Listen with interest – you may learn more than you think!

❋ Be aware of any special needs the older people in your
family may have and use good manners to help them.

Manners
All Around

When someone says something nice about you, say "Thank you".

✳ It's also nice to return a compliment when possible.

✳ Making eye contact is good manners.

✳ Accept the nice words and never say, "I know that."

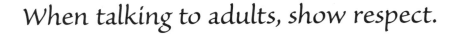

When talking to adults, show respect.

* When talking to adults, use a respectful name, such as "Mr." or "Ms." or "Aunt" or "Uncle", etc.

* Call an adult by his/her first name only if you are told to do so.

* Don't interrupt when adults are talking.

Step back and offer to hold the door for other people entering public places.

* Notice when other people may need your help.

* Remember – young children and older adults may have problems opening heavy doors.

* Be aware of people using wheelchairs or crutches and hold doors for them to enter first.

Use good manners in crowded places.

❋ Take your time when moving from place to place.

❋ Wait for your turn patiently.

❋ Running in crowded places is rude.

Practice good listening skills in public places.

✱ Wait your turn before speaking (unless it is an emergency).

✱ To listen is to respect.

✱ Good manners listens instead of interrupting.

Only enter or exit through proper doors.

❋ Never enter places that are not marked.

❋ Never enter places that have signs with "Employees Only".

Things to remember in public places.

❋ It is nice to remove your hat when inside a building.

❋ Never enter places that have signs "Employees Only".

❋ Unnecessary noises in public are poor manners.

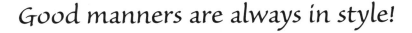

Good manners are always in style!

❋ Clean clothes are a must!

❋ Dressing neatly fits everyone.

❋ Clean hair is always "in"!

Good manners never use dirty words like …

* Messy clothes.

* Grimy hands and face.

* Ugly words.

You should stand quietly and respectfully during "Moments of Silence".

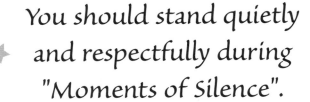

* At school

* Before ball games

* At special programs

Good manners involve conservation.

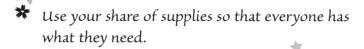 Use your share of supplies so that everyone has what they need.

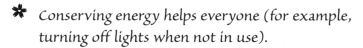 Conserving energy helps everyone (for example, turning off lights when not in use).

Practice conservation by using good manners with clothes, food, toys, and other items your parents have provided you.

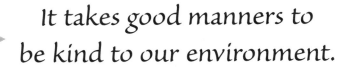

It takes good manners to be kind to our environment.

❋ Throwing litter in rivers and oceans harms animals like ducks and sea turtles.

❋ Our environment is precious – use good manners to help preserve it.

❋ Doing your part to help protect our environment is the right thing to do.

Inviting others should include good manners.

❋ Only take invitations to school if everyone in your class is being invited.

❋ Be sure that no one around you feels left out.

❋ Plan carefully.

Good winners have good manners.

* Be a good sport at sports.

* Be an encouraging winner to others.

* Good winners respect the efforts of everyone.

Good manners respect the privacy of others.

✳ Sometimes people want to be alone.

✳ Be aware there are some things people do not want to talk about in front of others.

✳ Other people's grades, mail, and conversations are private.

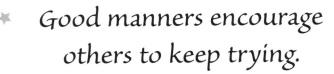

Good manners encourage others to keep trying.

❋ Tell someone what they do right – not what they do wrong.

❋ Sincere compliments help others to keep trying.

❋ Build others up, never tear them down!

Good Manners On Giving & Receiving Gifts

Use your best manners when someone gives you a gift.

❋ Say "thank you" in a voice that lets the giver know you mean it.

❋ It's not polite to ask how much something cost.

❋ Don't ask where the gift was purchased.

❋ Unkind remarks about the gift or the way it was wrapped are not showing good manners.

When someone gives you a gift
you don't like, or you already have
one: simply say " Thank you " in a
sincere, pleasant tone of voice
with a happy look on your face.

✱ After all, it is the kind thought that really counts!

✱ Saying "I already have one of these" is a hurtful
statement to the giver.

✱ Good manners never include statements such as, "I don't like
this" or "This isn't what I wanted" or "What's this for? Are those
statements you'd like to hear when you give someone a gift?

Day 132

The person giving the gift has spent time and money choosing a gift just for you!

* Always write a thank you note as quickly as possible after receiving gifts

* Be thankful that someone wanted to remember you with a gift.

* Be sincere with your thanks.

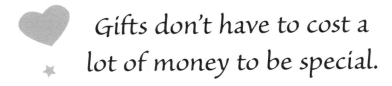

Gifts don't have to cost a lot of money to be special.

❋ Don't worry about what other people are giving—
your gift is special because it came from you.

❋ Good manners never include telling the person
how much you paid for the gift.

❋ If you are asked where the gift was purchased,
it's a good idea to simply say, "I picked it out in
a special store just for you."

You can show good manners by saying "Thank You" in different ways.

* You can phone someone to say "thank you".

* You can say thank you in person (face-to-face).

* Everyone appreciates a "thank you" note.

Use good manners when writing "Thank You" notes.

❋ Write a "Thank You" note to the giver as soon as possible.

❋ Start the note by telling that person how much you appreciated the gift, and be sure to include the name of the gift.

❋ Include one or two sentences that lets the giver know how much you appreciate their thoughtfulness in remembering you in such a special way.

❋ Close the note pleasantly such as "Your friend," or "Yours truly," or even   "Love," if it was from a very special person and be sure to sign your name.

Manners
In Your
Neighborhood

Always ask permission before going through a neighbor's yard.

✳ There could be a mean dog.

✳ You might damage property (such as plants).

✳ You could be mistaken for a burglar.

Use good manners by understanding loud noises bother some people.

❋ Music should be played at a medium tone,
   not a loud volume.

❋ Be aware of the times neighbors rest (i.e. early morning
   or late at night are not times for loud noises).

❋ Loud vehicles (such as 4-wheelers, dirt bikes, etc.) should
   be ridden in places that do not disturb neighbors.

Help keep your neighborhood neat and clean.

❋ Pick up trash in your yard.

❋ Be sure to put your trash in the correct trash container – never litter the streets.

❋ Help make sure lids on outside trash cans are closed tightly.

Use good manners when visiting neighbors.

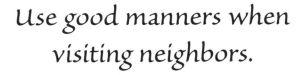

❋ Try to call before visiting neighbors.

❋ If visiting at meal time, ask if it would
  be better to come back later.

❋ Only ring the doorbell or knock on the
  door one or two times.

Good manners complement – never criticize where someone else lives.

🌸 The size of someone's house.

🌸 The kind of furniture.

🌸 The type of house they live in (such as apartment, mobile home, etc.).

Good manners are important with neighborhood friends.

✱ If your neighborhood friend already has a guest,
  it's not good manners to stay without being invited.

✱ Only get something to eat or drink after asking politely first.

✱ Be understanding of younger children in your neighborhood.

Use good manners by respecting your neighbor's property.

❋ Decorations should be looked at, not touched or moved.

❋ Always ask before moving anything that belongs to your neighbor (bikes, tools, etc.).

❋ Plants and flowers are beautiful and should not be bothered with permission.

Respect other people's pets.

❋ Animals are often loved similar to members of the family.

❋ Feeding your neighbor's pets, without permission, is never a good idea.

❋ Some pets bite when they are frightened.

Spreading neighborhood gossip is not kind.

* Gossip can cause arguments.

* Gossip can hurt feelings.

* Gossip can harm a person's reputation.

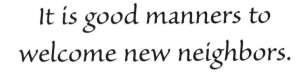

It is good manners to welcome new neighbors.

✱ Always with an adult, it is nice to introduce yourself to new neighbors.

✱ Take them some food.

✱ Offer to help them while moving into their new home.

Good
Manners in the
United States
of America

Respect our country's national traditions.

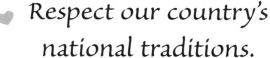

❊ Respect the meaning and history of the flag.

❊ It is good manners to respect other people's love for our country.

❊ Respect people who have served in the past or who are serving now in our military.

It is good manners and respectful
to obey the laws of our nation.

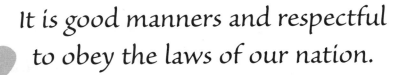

❋ Respecting and obeying the laws of ….

❋ The town where you live helps make up a better state….

❋ Which helps make our country a better place.

It is good manners to
respect the people who are in
governmental leadership positions.

* It is good manners to respect the Mayor of your town.

* It is good manners to respect the Governor of your state.

* The office of the President of our country should have our respect.

It is good manners to recognize every citizen's right to choose.

❋ Voting is a free choice.

❋ You can disagree with someone and still be polite.

❋ You can be kind, yet firm, in your beliefs.

Recognizing our personal freedoms

* religion/opinion

* schools

* sports

Good
Manners
and Good
Character

Practicing good manners is your individual responsibility.

* No matter what others do you can have good manners.

* The choice is always YOURS!

* Responsibility is maturity.

Honesty and good manners go hand in hand.

✻ Being honest does not mean being rude – ever!

✻ Others will respect your honesty.

✻ Honesty helps you remember your manners.

Good manners always involve kindness.

* Kindness is appreciated by everyone.

* Kindness is needed in every situation.

* Kindness is ageless.

Good manners build trust.

🌸 Good manners help others trust you more.

🌸 When you are trusted, you are given more freedom to do more things.

🌸 Trust is mutual – it's a bond between two or more people that should never be broken.

Good manners = Good reputation!

* Your reputation is like your shadow.

* Good or bad – the choice is yours – the reputation is yours!

* A good reputation is something that grows with you.

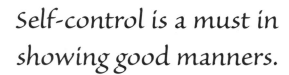

Self-control is a must in showing good manners.

* There is no place when practicing good manners for temper tantrums.

* Self-control is needed when we are tired.

* Self-control helps you focus.

Gentleness is a part of good manners.

* Gentleness is needed with other people.

* Gentleness is needed when caring for animals.

* Use gentleness when using things that belong to others.

Good manners involve patience.

* Being patient helps us think before we act.

* Being patient sets a good example.

* Good manners and patience belong together.

A good attitude results in good manners.

* Positive thinking means proper manners.

* Everyone benefits from a good attitude.

* Good attitude, good manners, good results!

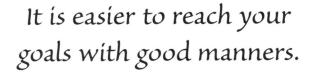

It is easier to reach your goals with good manners.

* If your goal is to have more friends, good manners is the key.

* If your goal is to have a good school year, good manners with others will help you get there!

* If your goal is to live a more successful life, living and choosing good manners will help you!

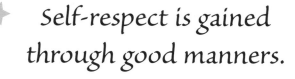

Self-respect is gained through good manners.

✱ You will like yourself, as well as others will enjoy you if you practice good manners.

✱ Better choices, better manners, better self-respect!

✱ Feeling better about yourself means more self-respect.

Punctuality is a part of good manners.

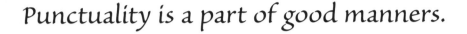

* Being punctual means being on time.

* Keeping others waiting is not using good manners.

* Being on time helps you build a good reputation
for yourself.

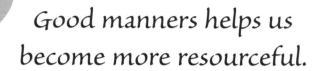

Good manners helps us become more resourceful.

❋ Being resourceful helps us think of better ways to accomplish our goals when the first way we try does not work.

❋ Being resourceful can help us in many ways and in many situations.

❋ Being resourceful is important when you are faced with situations that are difficult to practice good manners.

Tolerance of other's differences shows good manners.

* Being tolerant of the ideas of others is showing good manners.

* Realize your way is not the only way!

* Be tolerant of the beliefs of others – this is practicing good manners.

Good manners includes humility.

❋ Being humble means not bragging.

❋ Bragging is not practicing good manners!

❋ Humility is the opposite of being too proud.

Sometimes diligence is needed to practice good manners.

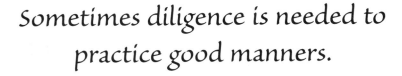

❋ Being diligent means continuing to practice something even when it is hard to do so.

❋ By not giving up on good manners, you have stayed strong!

❋ Make up your mind that no matter what, you will stay diligent and exercise good manners!

Hospitality welcomes good manners.

❋ When you practice using hospitality, you make your guests feel welcome

❋ Hospitality helps everyone feel comfortable.

❋ Practicing hospitality makes others want to be around you.

Being sensitive to others fosters good manners.

✻ Being sensitive and aware of the needs of others shows good manners.

✻ The feelings of others are an area where good manners are a must!

✻ Certain situations require sensitivity – use your good manners and help things run more smoothly for everyone concerned.

At times we must be flexible when practicing good manners.

* When you are in a group, allow yourself to be flexible.
* When your plans need to be changed, flexibility is a must.
* When someone has a different idea, it may be necessary to bend a little.

Using good manners sometimes involves courage.

❋ Being polite in most situations involves courage.

❋ Using good manners when those around you are not takes courage.

❋ It takes time and courage to change old habits.

You can expect good manners from dependable people.

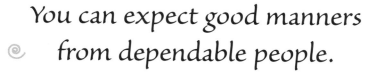

❋ Dependable people are mannerly people.

❋ Dependable people can be trusted.

❋ Good friends stay that way because they can depend on each other to act properly.

Be determined to have good manners!

* Determine to choose good manners.

* Be determined to learn and practice good manners.

* Be determined on good AND bad days to practice good manners.

Good manners contribute to peacefulness.

❋ People react better and more peacefully when everyone practices good manners.

❋ People are happier with you when you practice good manners.

❋ You can be more peaceful inside when you have chosen to use good manners.

Friendships involve good manners.

❋ Friends aren't rude to friends!

❋ Friends say "please" and "thank you", too!

❋ Good attitudes + Good Manners = Good Friends

Good manners take cooperation at times.

* It is good manners to share.

* It takes good manners to work along with other people.

* Teamwork involves good manners.

Good manners avoid unnecessary conflict.

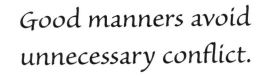

* Try to understand both opinions.

* If you cannot agree, using a soft voice
  and kind words may help the situation.

* Kindness and good manners help avoid arguments.

Good manners help forgiveness to take place more easily.

✱ Good manners accept, "I am sorry."

✱ Good manners say, "I am sorry."

✱ Good manners don't hold grudges.

Be responsible for your own mistakes.

❋ Don't blame others for your mistakes.

❋ Learn from your mistakes.

❋ Accept the consequences of your actions.

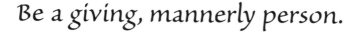

Be a giving, mannerly person.

❋ Give of your time to help others.

❋ Give of your talents (things you are good at) to help others.

❋ Give your attention when others are speaking, performing, or requesting help.

About the Authors...

Donna Forrest is the author of 180 Days of Character, Character Under Construction, and the co-author of Developmental Guidance Activities. She has experience as a classroom teacher, school counselor, and works part time in private practice. Donna has an Educational Specialist degree in Counselor Education from the University of South Carolina, is a Licensed Professional Counselor in South Carolina and Georgia, and a National Certified Counselor.

Jenny Menger has taught elementary children in various grade levels for 17 years. She is a graduate of the University of South Carolina in Aiken and is well-known for her expertise in both interior and floral design. She is called upon frequently to plan dinner parties and give advice in the areas of etiquette and manners.